The Ripple Effect

Environmental Impacts Of Plant-based Milk.

BY
JOEL HUNTER

INTRODUCTION

The environmental difficulties confronting our globe today are unparalleled. The issues affecting our civilization include resource depletion, habitat loss, and climate change. But when it comes to environmental damage, the dairy sector is one of the most disregarded. Dairy has a significant negative environmental effect, including land degradation, greenhouse gas emissions, and water consumption. There is nevertheless hope.

The emergence of vegan dairy substitutes has completely changed the game. The demand for dairy milk is falling as more people choose a plant-based diet, and this trend has far-reaching effects. This book investigates the environmental benefits of plant milk. We examine the various advantages of converting to plant-based milk, including the economics of dairy farming as well as the effects on the environment and public health.

TABLE OF CONTENT

Chapter 1: The dairy industry's Effects on the Environment

The ecology is greatly impacted by the dairy sector. There are significant environmental costs associated with dairy products, including greenhouse gas emissions, water usage, and soil degradation. For instance, in the US, dairy cows produce 1.4 billion tons of greenhouse gases annually, which is more than 290 million automobiles' worth of emissions. Calculations reveal that the manufacture of dairy products uses a significant amount of water, with one liter of milk requiring almost 1,000 gallons of water.

The dairy sector contributes to land degradation and deforestation, in addition to having an impact on the climate and water supplies. Large tracts of land must be set aside for cattle to graze, which threatens ecosystems and the environment.

In addition, using pesticides and fertilizers for dairy crops may pollute water supplies and soils, furthering the state of the environment. Consumers should be aware of the dairy industry's negative effects on the environment and weigh their options. We may drastically lessen our environmental impact and help ensure a sustainable future by selecting plant-based dairy substitutes.

The emotional effect of the dairy industry's environmental impact must be understood. As we grow more conscious of the effects of our activities, it may be daunting to consider the harm we are causing to the earth. But it's important to keep in mind that things might change. Making simple changes, such as selecting dairy products made from plants, may have a significant impact.

The environment consists of more than simply a collection of usable materials. It is a dynamic system that sustains all forms of life on Earth. We hurt the environment when we do something bad to ourselves or the next generation. The dairy industry's effects on the environment go beyond numbers and figures. It is up to us to take action since we feel a heavy burden of duty for the world and our future.

Making the switch to plant-based milk may help. We can preserve water, lessen our carbon footprint, and safeguard the ecosystem. We may have an impact that goes beyond our own decisions. Although the dairy business often seems like an overwhelming obstacle, even the smallest decision we make may have a significant influence.

So let's confidently and with pride pick plant-based milk. Accept the emotional weight of this decision and find solace in the notion that we are evolving. Real consequences result from selecting plant-based milk, and by doing so, we improve both our futures and the future of the world.

We also choose compassion when we select plant-based milk. We decide to promote a humane society and lessen animal suffering. Poor animal management, including removing calves from their mothers and cramming animals in small places, is a common practice in the dairy business. We make the ethical decision to reject this brutality by promoting plant-based dairy substitutes.

It's not, however, about animals. Humans are also affected by this. Farmers and employees who operate in the dairy business may be subjected to hazardous chemicals and go through financial hardship as a result. To contribute to a just and sustainable food system, choose plant-based milk. You can run across opposition from others if you convert to plant-based milk.

Some people may find it difficult or even impossible to give up dairy. But we must always keep in mind that every action counts as development. By educating ourselves and others on the advantages of plant-based milk, we can encourage kinder and more environmentally friendly lives. The choice to transition to plant-based milk is ultimately a personal one. It is both an emotional and logical decision. It's about accepting responsibility for our part in improving the world and being aware of the effects our activities have on the environment, animals, and people.

The advantages of plant milk will be covered in more detail in the next chapter of this book. We explore the various advantages of plant milk, including its positive effects on the environment and its health benefits. They consider the future of food and agriculture as well as the dairy industry's effects on the environment. By working together, we can improve the world one glass of plant-based milk at a time.

Chapter 2: The Health Advantages of Plant-Based Milk.

There are other health benefits to take into account, in addition to the environmental advantages of plant-based milk substitutes. Providing a variety of vitamins and minerals without the cholesterol and saturated fat found in dairy milk, plant-based milk substitutes may be a delightful and healthy supplement to any diet.

The reduced saturated fat level of plant-based milk substitutes is one of their key advantages. Heart disease, stroke, and diabetes are just a few of the health issues that have been related to saturated fat. We may lower our consumption of saturated fat and encourage a healthy diet by opting for plant-based milk substitutes.

Additionally, plant-based milk substitutes are often enriched with vitamins and minerals like calcium and vitamin D, which are crucial for keeping healthy bones and teeth. Many plant-based milk substitutes are also low in calories and sugar, which makes them an excellent choice for anyone trying to control their diabetes or maintain a healthy weight.

Plant-based milk substitutes provide a welcome option for people who are lactose intolerant or allergic to dairy products. These dairy substitutes do not induce the gastrointestinal discomfort that might come with dairy intake and are often simpler to digest.

Additionally, plant-based milk substitutes come in a variety of mouthwatering and cutting-edge tastes, from creamy oat milk to rich almond milk. They are a useful asset to any kitchen and may be used in a wide range of dishes.

In conclusion, plant-based milk substitutes are a wise option for anyone trying to encourage a better diet since they provide several health advantages. The various advantages of plant-based milk substitutes will be thoroughly discussed in the chapters to follow, along with the future of agriculture and food.

Chapter 3: The Ethics of Plant-Based Milk.

Concerns about animal welfare and the management of dairy cows have long fueled discussions about the ethics of the dairy business. Another contentious topic is the use of hormones and antibiotics in dairy production. For people who are worried about the treatment of animals and the use of antibiotics and hormones in food production, plant-based milk replacements provide a more moral option.

In order to boost milk output, dairy cows are often exposed to intensive agricultural techniques, such as hormone and antibiotic treatments. Both people and cows may have health issues as a result of these procedures, which also raise the risk of antibiotic resistance. Additionally, the dairy business often separates mother cows from their calves soon after delivery, a process that may be upsetting for both the cow and the baby.

Contrarily, plant-based milk substitutes don't employ animals and don't add to the ethical issues connected to the dairy business. In addition to being more sustainable and ecologically benign, the manufacture of plant-based milk substitutes also uses less water, land, and other resources.

By selecting plant-based milk substitutes, we can support moral and environmentally friendly food production methods and advance a better future for animals and the environment. We shall examine the many ethical issues surrounding food production and take into account the future of agriculture and food in the chapters that follow.

Chapter 4: The Economic Benefits of Plant-Based Milk.

Plant-based milk substitutes may boost the economy in addition to providing health and environmental advantages. Farmers and food producers have a wide range of business options to consider as consumer demand for plant-based milk substitutes rises.

Jobs in agriculture and food processing may be created as a result of the manufacturing of plant-based milk substitutes, strengthening local economies and fostering expansion. Additionally, compared to dairy farming, the manufacturing of plant-based milk substitutes uses less water and land, which may lower costs and boost productivity.

Plant-based milk substitutes are a good option for farmers that want to diversify their crops and increase market share. Farmers now have the chance to investigate new directions for development and innovation as well as to develop new goods that satisfy customer demand thanks to the industry's expansion for plant-based milk.

Additionally, the greater accessibility and acceptance of plant-based milk substitutes may boost competition in the market for dairy goods, resulting in reduced pricing for consumers and better access to a variety of nutritious food choices.

By selecting plant-based milk substitutes, we can help the food sector develop sustainably and creatively and improve the economic health of our communities. In the chapters that follow, we'll delve further into the many financial advantages of plant-based milk substitutes and look forward to the state of food and agriculture.

Chapter 5: The Cultural Importance of Plant-Based Milk.

Food and drink are often inextricably linked to cultural identity and customs. The chance to discover and appreciate a broad range of cultural and culinary traditions from throughout the globe is provided by plant-based milk substitutes.

For instance, soy milk has been a common ingredient in many East Asian cultures for a very long time, while almond milk has long been a part of Middle Eastern and Mediterranean cooking. Coconut milk and cashew milk are popular plant-based milk substitutes in South Asia for baking and cooking.

In addition, as chefs and food manufacturers experiment with novel ingredients and methods, the rising popularity of plant-based milk substitutes has sparked the development of fresh culinary and cultural traditions. As a consequence, the food environment is varied and interesting, offering limitless opportunities for experimentation and invention in the kitchen.

Additionally, plant-based milk substitutes may foster a deeper appreciation and understanding of other cultures and customs by assisting in the removal of cultural barriers. Investigating the cultural importance of plant-based milk substitutes might help us better appreciate and value the vast variety of the environment we live in.

By selecting plant-based milk substitutes, we may honor local customs and foster better respect and awareness among many groups. In the chapters that follow, we will delve further into the cultural relevance of plant-based milk substitutes and look forward to the state of food and agriculture.

Chapter 6: The Ethical Considerations of Plant-Based Milk

As a result of their ethical concerns about animal welfare and environmental sustainability, many individuals are attracted to plant-based milk substitutes. Due to the dairy industry's effects on animal welfare and the environment, it has recently come under growing criticism, and many customers are searching for alternatives that are more in line with their beliefs.

Traditional dairy products may be replaced with cruelty-free, sustainable plant-based milk substitutes. We may lessen our dependence on the dairy sector and contribute to a humane and sustainable food system by selecting plant-based milk substitutes.

Additionally, since it uses less water, land, and resources than dairy farming, the manufacturing of plant-based milk substitutes is often more ecologically benign than dairy farming. This can support a more sustainable future for our world by lowering the carbon footprint of the food business.

Additionally, because dairy cows no longer need to be forcefully impregnated and removed from their calves, the manufacturing of plant-based milk substitutes may help lessen animal abuse. This may improve animal welfare and foster a culture that values compassion.

We may make dietary choices that are consistent with our moral principles and advance a more humane and sustainable future by selecting plant-based milk substitutes. We will delve further into the ethical issues surrounding plant-based milk substitutes and take a look at the future of agriculture and food in the chapters to follow.

Chapter 7: The Health Advantages of Plant-Based Milk

In addition to being good for the environment and the welfare of animals, plant-based milk substitutes also provide several health advantages. Plant-based milk substitutes provide a secure and nutritious substitute for conventional dairy products for those who are lactose intolerant or have a milk allergy.

In addition, a lot of plant-based milk substitutes are packed with vitamins and minerals including calcium, vitamin D, and protein. Particularly for people who eat a vegan or vegetarian diet, this may enhance general health and well-being.

Additionally, it has been shown that plant-based milk substitutes have less fat than conventional dairy goods, which may help to decrease cholesterol levels and a person's risk of developing heart disease.

By selecting plant-based milk substitutes, we may promote our health and well-being and help create a more humane and sustainable food system. The health advantages of plant-based milk substitutes will be further discussed in the chapters that

follow, along with the future of agriculture
and food.

Chapter 8: The Culinary Possibilities of Plant-Based Milk

A wide range of culinary options is opened up by plant-based milk substitutes, from making velvety sauces to baking delectable pastries. These plant-based substitutes' adaptability is extremely astonishing and may give our baking and cooking a whole new dimension.

Plant-based milk substitutes' neutral flavor, which enables its usage in a range of recipes without changing the flavor, is one advantage. As a result, they may easily be used in place of dairy milk in a variety of recipes, particularly those that call for a creamy texture.

Additionally, vitamin and mineral fortification makes plant-based milk substitutes a nutritious complement to our meals. Whether we use almond milk in our favorite smoothie or oat milk in our daily coffee, plant-based milk substitutes are a tasty and healthful alternative to conventional dairy products.

By investigating the gastronomic potential of plant-based milk substitutes, we may give our baking and cooking a fresh perspective while simultaneously promoting a more humane and sustainable food system. In the chapters that follow, we'll delve further into the culinary applications of plant-based milk substitutes and look forward to the state of agriculture and food production.

Chapter 9: Food and Agriculture in the Future

Future food and agricultural production is a complicated and critical subject that has to be addressed immediately. It is obvious that we need to rethink our food systems and implement more humane and sustainable methods in light of the expanding global population and mounting environmental sustainability problems.

Milk alternatives made from plants provide a viable answer to many of these problems. We can lessen our carbon footprint and promote more ethical and ecological agricultural methods by lowering our dependence on conventional dairy products.

Additionally, plant-based milk substitutes provide a solution to meet the nutritional demands of our expanding population while lessening the detrimental effects of animal products on human health. We can promote our health and well-being and help create a more humane and sustainable food system by adopting a more plant-based diet.

But it will need group effort and cooperation from all facets of society to create a more humane and sustainable food system. It will need adjustments to governmental regulations, consumer habits, and business procedures. To tackle one of the most important issues of our time, the whole world will need to join together.

By accepting plant-based milk substitutes, we can make a huge step toward a more humane and sustainable future. The future of food and agriculture is in our hands. The future of food and agriculture will be thoroughly examined in the chapters that follow, and we'll also look at how plant-based milk substitutes could contribute to this revolutionary change.

Chapter 10: Embracing a Future That Is More Sustainable and Compassionate

It takes more than merely using cutting-edge agricultural techniques or new technology to secure the future of food and agriculture. It involves adopting a more humane and environmentally friendly method of producing, distributing, and consuming food.

The interdependence of all living things and the need of fostering a more amicable interaction between people, animals, and the environment is at the core of this strategy. It is about accepting responsibility for improving a more fair and equitable food system for all people and the effects of our decisions.

Alternatives to animal milk that are made from plants are a potent instrument for realizing this goal of a more humane and sustainable future. We can lessen the environmental effect of food production and encourage more moral and compassionate agricultural methods by consuming fewer animal products.

Additionally, plant-based milk substitutes provide a means of promoting everyone's health and well-being, independent of their dietary choices or cultural background. They provide a means of bridging gaps and encouraging a deeper appreciation of the variety of life on our planet.

It is obvious that we must modify our food systems in a bold and revolutionary way as we move into the future. Justice, compassion, and sustainability must become our new top objectives. We must adopt a more all-encompassing and integrated strategy for food production and consumption that values all living things.

We can make a significant step towards this more sustainable and humane future by adopting plant-based milk substitutes. Food that is not only healthy and tasty but also morally and environmentally sound may be created. We have the power to bring about a society in which all living things are appreciated and respected and where the health and welfare of both people and the environment come first.

In the chapters that follow, we'll go into more depth about the many advantages of plant-based milk substitutes and think about how they could contribute to a future that is more compassionate and sustainable for everyone.

Chapter 11: Meeting Obstacles and Developing Resilience

It's critical to understand that the path to a more humane and sustainable future won't be simple. There will be difficulties, failures, and times of uncertainty and annoyance. But it's exactly during these times that we need to muster our fortitude and resiliency and devise fresh strategies for getting forward.

Resistance to change is one of the major problems we have. Many individuals may find it challenging to embrace the concept of avoiding conventional animal-based goods, particularly when it comes to something as basic as milk. Accepting something new and different while letting go of old habits and preferences may be difficult.

Truth be told, change is unavoidable. We must be prepared to change along with our society and the earth as they continue to develop. For a future that is more humane and sustainable, we must be prepared to put our presumptions and beliefs to the test.

Our complicated food system is another difficulty we encounter. It may be challenging to identify and solve the primary causes of issues due to the interdependence between agriculture, industry, politics, and culture. Trying to traverse this complexity and come up with solutions that are both efficient and fair may be intimidating.

But we must persist. We must keep asking questions, looking for knowledge and resources, and cooperating to discover answers. To bring about significant change, we must empower ourselves and others by establishing networks of cooperation and support.

We may find courage and motivation in the many triumphs and achievements of individuals who have gone before us as we confront these difficulties. We stand on the shoulders of giants, from the forerunners of the plant-based milk business to the activists and supporters who have pushed for animal rights and environmental conservation.

Additionally, we may rely on one another for strength. We can create a movement that is strong and transformational by exchanging our experiences and stories, providing support and encouragement, and cooperating to achieve a shared objective.

We will examine some of the doable actions we can take to get over these obstacles and create a more resilient and compassionate future in the book's concluding chapters. We will examine the roles that lobbying, education, and policy play in bringing about change and provide advice on how to live our everyday lives using plant-based milk substitutes. Above all, we will honor the value of optimism and tenacity in the face of hardship as well as the strength of group effort.

Chapter 12: The Influence of Advocacy and Education

Two of the most effective instruments we have for bringing about significant change are education and advocacy. We may encourage people to act and change things by improving knowledge of the problems associated with environmental sustainability and animal agribusiness.

However, advocacy and education may be difficult as well. Finding the appropriate language and communication techniques to successfully reach people may be challenging and frustrating when dealing with resistance or apathy.

We must keep going, nonetheless, despite these obstacles. In our attempts to spread knowledge and fight for a more compassionate and sustainable society, we must be persistent, patient, and kind.

Focusing on similar beliefs and experiences is one of the keys to efficient lobbying and education. We have a better chance of bringing about significant change when we can engage people on a deeper level and demonstrate the connection between the problems we care about and their own lives and beliefs.

To connect with various audiences, we might use a range of tactics and methods. There are a variety of methods to inform and advocate for change, including social media campaigns, neighborhood gatherings, and one-on-one interactions.

Perhaps most significantly, we must also be willing to develop as people and learn new things. We must be open to hearing diverse points of view and incorporating suggestions and criticism into our work. To build settings where everyone may feel empowered to make a difference, we must work to be welcoming, inclusive, and inclusive.

The role that policy and regulation play in establishing a more sustainable and kind food system will be discussed in the next chapter. We will examine how rules and regulations may influence our decisions and actions and talk about tactics for promoting policy change. We can create a world where plant-based milk is the norm and where sustainability and compassion are at the forefront of our dietary choices via education, activism, and legislation.

Chapter 13: The Influence of Regulation and Policy

Individual decisions and actions have a significant role in developing a more sustainable and compassionate food system, as we have seen throughout this book. However, we can't depend just on individual actions to bring about the systemic transformation we need. In order to build a more equitable and sustainable society, we must also consider policy and regulation as potent weapons.

We can encourage the production of healthy, compassionate foods via laws and regulations, and we can hold businesses responsible for their effects on the environment and animal welfare. As an example, we can assist the production of plant-based milk by passing legislation that makes it simpler and cheaper for consumers to make decisions that are consistent with their beliefs.

Making progress on policy reform, however, may be challenging because of how complicated and stressful the political process can be. Observing business lobbyists and other special interests fighting against the needs of the earth and its people may be depressing.

However, we must not give up. We must keep pushing for policy modifications and holding our elected leaders responsible for their deeds. Through nonviolent protests, open rallies, and other kinds of group action, we must share our opinions.

Additionally, we must acknowledge that changing policy is not the sole option. In addition to supporting the creation of compassionate and sustainable local and regional food systems, we must continue to focus on changing cultural norms and individual behavior.

In the end, developing a more compassionate and sustainable society requires a multidimensional strategy that combines individual action, lobbying, education, and legislative reform. We can work together to build a society where plant-based milk is the norm and where compassion and sustainability guide our dietary choices.

It's crucial to keep in mind that changing policies may be a potent weapon for bringing about the change we desire as we go forward on our path toward a world that is more sustainable and compassionate. Policy and regulation may have a significant and enduring influence on not just our own lives but also the lives of future generations.

It may be upsetting to see how individuals who value money above people and the environment impede development. But we must persist in our fight for change, holding people in positions of authority responsible and promoting laws that put compassion and sustainability first.

We have the ability to improve the world for all creatures when we band together to fight for policy change. Seeing the results of our group efforts and realizing that we are changing the world may be inspiring.

However, changing the law is not the sole option. Recognizing the strength of our everyday decisions and the influence they have on the world around us, we must also continue to work on changing individual behavior and societal trends.

Let's keep working toward a future where plant-based milk is the norm and sustainability and compassion are at the forefront of our food chain while keeping optimism in our hearts as we go ahead. In order to build a world where all creatures may flourish and where our actions have a positive ripple effect that promotes compassion, love, and respect for all life, let's employ the power of policy and regulation.

Plant-based milk has a genuinely amazing ripple effect. Every time we choose to use it in place of animal milk, we are expressing our preferences for the sort of society we want to live in. a future where the wellbeing of our planet is of utmost importance and where the pain of animals is not downplayed or normalized.

The size of the problems we confront, from climate change to animal welfare concerns, may make it simple to feel overpowered. But each time we choose to drink plant-based milk consciously, we are making a little but important step toward bringing about the change we want to see in the world.

It is not simple to move toward a world that is more compassionate and sustainable. It calls for bravery, tenacity, and a strong feeling of compassion for all living things. The benefits of this voyage, however, are immense. Animals are no longer seen as commodities in a society where plant-based milk is the norm. Our health and the health of the earth are given priority, and our actions have a positive ripple effect that benefits all living things.

Remember that change begins with us as we continue on this road. Every time we select plant-based milk, we are taking a little but significant step toward the world we want to live in. We have the capacity to build the world we desire. So let's keep making thoughtful decisions, pushing for reform, and working to create a future that is humane and sustainable for all living things.

The ability to choose has a genuinely transforming quality. Every time we decide to drink plant-based milk, we are expressing our priorities and our beliefs. We have decided to promote a more sustainable and compassionate society that puts the welfare of all living things first.

When there is so much pain and devastation, it is simple to feel useless. When we read the news about issues like animal abuse, deforestation, and climate change, we question what we can do to help. However, the fact is that by choosing plant-based milk, we are fighting these injustices every time. Instead of adding to the issue, we have made the decision to be a part of the solution.

It is quite amazing how our decisions have repercussions. We help farmers who are trying to build a more sustainable food system every time we select plant-based milk. We are lowering our carbon footprint and assisting in the reduction of climate change's disastrous repercussions. Additionally, we are defending the rights of animals, who should be treated with compassion and respect.

However, the effects of our decisions go well beyond these brief advantages. By selecting plant-based milk, we are also telling the world what type of future we want to build. We are communicating to our loved ones that we are concerned about the condition of our planet and the welfare of all living things. We are causing a chain reaction that goes far beyond our acts by encouraging people to make deliberate decisions.

So let's keep in mind the influence our decisions may have on the world we live in. Let's keep supporting a humane and sustainable society by choosing plant-based milk. Together, we can build a world that values compassion, love, and respect for all living things.

CONCLUSION

"The Ripple Effect: Environmental Impact of Plant-based Milk" clarifies an important facet of our worldwide sustainability initiatives, to sum up. We have examined the many environmental consequences of the plant-based milk business throughout this book, offering a thorough examination of its effects on the environment.

We've been through the many production phases, looking at crop cultivation, water consumption, land management, greenhouse gas emissions, and waste creation related to plant-based milk substitutes. The information given here emphasizes how important it is to take these into account when assessing how environmentally sustainable our eating choices are.

Comparing the production of plant-based milk to that of conventional dairy provides significant advantages. Plant-based milk production uses fewer resources, such as water and land, while producing a considerable reduction in greenhouse gas emissions. Additionally, the market for plant-based milk is poised to boost circularity and reduce waste output, which is encouraging steps toward a more sustainable future.

However, we must admit that there are no quick fixes for preserving the environment. While plant-based milk offers a practical substitute for conventional dairy products, its production must be approached with great care. Addressing possible problems like monoculture farming, deforestation, and the use of artificial inputs in agricultural growing s part of this. We can allay these worries and increase the advantages of plant-based milk by using ethical agricultural methods, managing our land sustainably, and using fewer non-renewable resources.

The movie "The Ripple Effect" calls for cooperation between legislators, business executives, academics, and consumers to promote the development of a viable plant-based milk market. We can create and improve procedures that reduce environmental damage and support a healthier, more environmentally aware society via education, creativity, and cooperation.

Inspiring people and organizations to see the potential of plant-based milk as a major instrument in the goal of a greener and more sustainable world is our ambition for this book, which we believe will spark real change. We may leave a good environmental legacy for future generations by realizing the effects of our decisions and embracing the power of informed decision-making.

Let "The Ripple Effect: Environmental Impact of Plant-based Milk" serve as a foundation for a day when making sustainable food choices is not just a luxury but also a basic human right. Together, we can create a society that balances our nutritional requirements with the health of the environment, leaving a beneficial legacy for future generations.

9 798395 051851